HIGH, LOW & WET

HIGH, LOW & WET

*Further Aircraft crashes in North Wales
and some coastal incidents*

Edward Doylerush

Front Cover Photographs:
Piper Tomahawk G-BOCC
on Elidir Fawr.
Lockheed P38F Lightning
41-7677 in sand near Harlech.
Sources in chapters.

First published in 2016

ISBN: 978-1-84524-248-0

Cover design: Michael G Thomas, MGT Design
www.edwarddoylerush.co.uk

Published by Gwasg Carreg Gwalch,
12 Iard yr Orsaf, Llanrwst, Wales LL26 0EH
tel: 01492 642031
fax: 01492 641502
email: books@carreg-gwalch.com
website: www.carreg-gwalch.com

This work is dedicated to the memory of all Royal Air Force, Commonwealth, and Allied airmen, Air Transport Auxiliary pilots, Air Training Corps cadets, and civilians who lost their lives in aircraft incidents in north Wales and in the sea beyond.

Contents

Foreword

In this latest book, *High, Low and Wet*, the enthusiasm for flying which is evident in all of Eddie Doylerush's acclaimed books comes to the fore once again. His research into accidents concerning aircraft in north Wales is extremely thorough, and his enthusiasm brings each incident to life and leaves a fitting legacy for all involved.

Eddie Doylerush's ambition to become a pilot in the Royal Air Force was thwarted due to the large numbers of aircrew remaining after World War II. Yet, instead of becoming disheartened and disillusioned, his passion spurred him on to uncover a variety of interesting and invariably exciting stories of aircraft crashes in his beloved North Wales. He has spent many years documenting and photographing the sites which has necessitated walking and climbing Snowdonia's craggy summits in search of these airframes.

Each chapter is written in a style that makes for easy reading: this book details the triumphs and disappointments encountered by those who, attracted by the challenges and thrills of flying, were fortunate enough to achieve their aim but unlucky enough to be involved in incidents, some of which, sadly, were fatal. Eddie's accounts include humour, pathos, and sensitivity as he deals with the various incidents and the crews involved. He has the extraordinary capacity of enabling the reader to be 'on the spot' thus giving the sense of being an eye witness. This is achieved by his thorough research into the incidents and his descriptive ability which brings the different terrains clearly into the imagination.

As I was a pilot in the RAF myself, I know the terrain he describes intimately and he has awakened vivid memories of sorties that I have flown, getting the adrenaline pumping once more.

This excellent book is a welcome addition to the others in the series he has written. I have no doubt that readers will enjoy Eddie Doylerush's *High, Low and Wet* as much as his earlier books.

Gp Capt Philip Langrill, OBE, RAF (Rtd).

Preface

With the drone of the non-synchronous engines of Luftwaffe bombers disturbing our evenings as they flew over Rhos-on-Sea to inflict terrible damage to Merseyside and Manchester early in the war, the writer felt that some personal response was due. This came late in 1942 when I turned fourteen and joined the Air Training Corps, Colwyn Bay County School's 1533 Flight. Aircraft recognition, identifying friend and foe was vital. Then came the Morse Code and navigation. Our splendid geography teacher, Mr E. Evans, was also our navigation instructor who taught us skills still remembered and useful today.

I had to wait impatiently for my first flight – in a Halifax bomber in June 1944 described in these pages, followed by a camp at RAF Mona in Anglesey where I flew in the Avro Ansons of No8 OAFU. Following the passing of the proficiency examination, I was given a gliding course at No 63 WEGS at Tal-y-cafn, on an alluvial plain south of Conway. At the end of 1946 I was summoned to register for call up in the transition to

Avro York RAF transport

National Service. To my dismay, aircrew were not required at that time, since so many were still being demobilised. Not wishing to be on airfields watching others fly decided me to go into the Army where, because of an interest in radio engineering, I was selected for REME and trained as a telecommunications mechanic. At the end of this long course I was offered a posting to West Germany. 'No Thank you' was my reply, we had bombed the place flat. Then I jumped at the alternative – West Africa, the White Man's Grave, adventure in the south. In December 1947 I was

Lee Boyd as 1st Officer on a B377 Stratocruiser at Idlewild, New York June 1956 (Alan Chalkley BOAC)

flown out in Avro York MW230 from RAF Manston in Kent to Castell Benito airfield in the desert south of Tripoli. A visit to the city showed a harbour full of sunken ships, masts and funnels poking above the waters.

Then on, in a night take off to Kano in northern Nigeria. We were flying over the Sahara at dawn when, after a glow in the east, the Sun shot like a shining sword above the horizon illuminating the huge sand dunes 8,000 feet below. After refuelling, we flew to Lagos over an increasing density of tropical forest. Our pilot, Flying Officer Lee Boyd DFC, thought to entertain us by dropping to almost tree top height. As we flew over clearings with their cluster of mud huts, people, goats and chickens ran this way and that as the huge noisy bird shot past. I climbed out of the York at

Lagos grass airfield to be nearly floored by the heat. I was still in battledress. Sergeant Major Craig from my new unit, No 1 Command Workshops, Yaba, saved me by whisking me into the bar for a pint of ice cool lager. I can taste it now.

We worked in the radio hut from 7.0 am till 1.0 pm. After lunch, an Army lorry would speed us to Victoria Beach near Lagos for the afternoon. For the princely sum of sixpence we could hire a plank cut to resemble a surf board, and spend a happy time cooling off in the sea. One afternoon I was standing with a board with my back to the sea, when a big wave shot up the beach, snatched my legs from under me and took me out to sea in the violent undertow. An indeterminate time later, I popped up like a cork into the daylight, gasping for breath. When I had composed myself I took stock of my position. I was on my own. There was no sign of life – only the Atlantic Ocean, by now no longer a playground. We had heard that a Royal Engineer officer had been taken by a shark out here a few months before, a worrisome thought. I had only learned to swim the previous summer, a gentle side stroke. No use for going far. After a while things were looking desperate when a higher than normal swell lifted me up. I then saw the tops of palm trees on the horizon. At last I had a direction to swim. However, I was rapidly tiring. The side stroke was not the powerful crawl. Suddenly I heard a sort of roar behind. Looking round I spied a giant Hawaiian type wave coming up on me. I put all my remaining strength into clawing my way up onto the crest as it arrived and was taken along at breakneck speed, to be dashed down on the beach at the feet of my chums. The lads were astounded at my sudden appearance but had the presence of mind to grab me before I vanished again.

The reason for this introduction is that it decided me to include a section on coastal losses. While I survived the experience, I can relate to others in a similar predicament with various outcomes. The sea can be an unforgiving host.

After all these years a thought came to me. How is it that with wind and longshore drift out in the ocean; that when I was brought ashore by the huge wave I landed exactly at the feet of my chums. Was it coincidence or was there some other force at work?

The book as a whole came about because over the years I found so much more information and quality photographs appeared to share with readers from previously sketchy beginnings. The Photofile section closes the work with photographs of aircrew and brief accounts of their accidents for posterity.

Acknowledgements

Group Captain Phil Langrill OBE for his sensitive and in depth foreword, also to his wife Joan for her contribution. Air Accident Investigation Branch, Colin Barber, Adrian Barrell, Doug Blair, Michael Collin, Librarians of Conwy Library.

Glyn Davies, Huw Edwards, Ken Ellis, Tom Ferris, Ric Gillespie & TIGHAR, Gwyn Hughes, Brian Jones, Neil Lewis, Chris Maddock, Ogwen Valley Mountain Rescue organisation, Simon W Parry, Judith Price, Glyn Pritchard, Gareth Pritchard, Tammy Richmond (niece), Matt Rimmer, David Roberts, John Ellis Roberts, David J Smith, Tim Stankus & Martin Skipworth of the Royal Signals Museum.

Alison Stevenson, Mel Thomas, Bernard Thomas, Geoff Wedge, Eric Westwood, Edgar Williams, Sqn Ldr Dave Williams, MCO, RAF Valley.

To my family members who made constant contributions: Wendy, Michael & Sian Thomas, Linda, Geoffrey, Sam, & Laura Wedge, and to my late wife Mary, for her support and for feeding the many visitors to our door.

Apologies to anyone omitted, your contributions are within and valuable to aviation history.

Edward Doylerush. Snowdonia 2015.

HIGH

First Flight – Final Flight

A Personal Chapter

First Flight

On 11th June 1944 a party of Air Training Corps cadets, of No. 1533 Flight (Colwyn Bay County School), including the writer, arrived at RAF Hawarden near Chester. This was a busy wartime airfield. An Operational Training Unit (OTU) for pilots was based here, indeed an unofficial Battle Flight of Spitfires was kept armed and at the ready. It claimed its first enemy aircraft with the downing of a Heinkel He 111 on 14th August 1940 near Saltney. The crew survived.

A shadow factory at the Broughton side produced Wellington bombers, changing over to Lancasters in 1944. It now produces wings for the acclaimed Airbus series.

Also based at Hawarden was No. 48 Maintenance Unit which stored new and repaired aircraft ready for delivery to squadrons as required.

After a mug of tea at the W.V.S wagon, our commanding officer, Flight Lieutenant Hobbs, called us together to advise that a Halifax bomber was going up on a test flight. All those who wanted to fly in it were to stand over at one side. He was nearly knocked down in the rush and had to pick six from the many. One of the youngest there, I must have looked so crestfallen that he decided that a miscount had taken place and sent me off to the parachute hut where I was helped into a harness, handed a parachute pack and instructed how to use it in an emergency.

Rounding the corner of a large hangar, I came upon

the great 'plane standing on a dispersal apron, all black, menacing, and guns a-bristling. One of the ground crew stood by a short ladder leading to an open door on the port side. I was first up the ladder and spotted the mid-upper turret above me. I scrambled up, nearly knocking myself out on a metal bar, and settled onto a metal seat. What a fine view I had. A pair of huge black wings seemed to stretch from horizon to horizon, ready to lift us into the air. As I swivelled round in the turret, the big rectangular tail fins came into view, just like a pair of barn doors.

My dream was shattered by a voice from below, and a tug at my heel. 'Come down from there'. A helmeted figure stood below. It was the pilot; a flight lieutenant. I dropped down out of the turret and sat with the other cadets at the side of the fuselage. Shortly after the pilot and flight engineer had gone forward, we heard the whine of a starter motor and the port outer engine burst into life, belching blue smoke. Like some primeval beast the Halifax slowly came to life. Each engine was run up in turn, then we felt the sudden lurch as the brakes were released and the aircraft rolled onto the perimeter track. In no time at all we were lined up at the start of the main runway, reaching away into infinity, and glistening after early morning rain.

I was at the peak of excitement with this my first flight. Taking off for the moon could not have held more in store. The roar of the engines increased to a crescendo while inside the dinosaur ten thousand vibrations were set up. I half expected the very rivets in the fuselage skin to start popping. The noise was quite deafening. How did crews cope with this hour after hour on long operational flights, taking in information on a hundred instruments, working out complex navigational problems, or just taking it in a gun turret?

The aircraft strained against the brakes, then a jerk forward as they were released and we were off. As we gathered speed the blades of grass at the side of the tarmac became a green blur. There was a slight tilting movement as the tail came up. The bumping and swaying suddenly ceased. We were airborne! As the pilot pulled back on the control column the cadets slid down the narrow seat against the rearmost cadet – me. Down below the fields were shrinking, the cattle in them becoming toys. We climbed at full bore until we reached the first wisps of cloud, then levelled off. Through the small window I could see the broad expanse of the Cheshire Plain. Then, as we turned, the Welsh Hills dark under lowering cloud. The 'plane started twisting and turning as the pilot put it though its paces. Sometimes we banked so steeply that we appeared to circle on a wing tip. At other times we seemed to fly over invisible humps where our stomachs were left on the peaks.

Then the note of the engines changed to a quieter pitch, coinciding with a sinking sensation. We were preparing to land. With the Dee Estuary ahead we flew the downwind leg parallel to the long runway, seemingly skimming a train on the railway. The tarmac rushed up to meet us, the pilot holding us off for a moment, then a screech from the tyres and we were safely down.

In the little flight hut the pilot filled in my new Flying Log book: **Hawarden. Halifax LW477 I.J.A Cruickshanks. Flt/ Lt. 30 mins 11 June 1944.**

Final Flight

Many years later, I decided to research the story of 'my' Halifax and see if I could find the pilot who had given me my first flight. Halifax Mk III, serial LW477 had been built by Handley Page at their Cricklewood factory and delivered to No. 158 Squadron at Lissett in Yorkshire on Christmas Eve 1943. On January 16th 1944 it was transferred to No. 640 (Canadian) Squadron. On the 23rd of the month Flying Officer Laidlaw was bringing the aircraft into land in a strong and gusty crosswind. He made a poor approach and instead of aborting and going round again he let her down. In doing so, the starboard rudder and wing tip hit the ground and he was extremely fortunate to regain control.

LW477 was out of commission until 1st June when it was flown to Hawarden to be held by No. 48 M.U. until required. Here I met it on its test flight, an experience I will always remember. Two days later it was delivered to No. 426 Squadron based at Linton-on-Ouse. The Canadians flew it on operations until mid-February 1945. It then had a major problem requiring repair at Handley Page workshops, possibly battle damage, the reason is not recorded. LW477 emerged at the end of May 1945, too late to continue to do battle. My pride and joy was ignominiously scrapped on 3rd July 1945.

My thoughts had often gone back to the pilot who took on that extra responsibility of a brood of cadets to give us flying experience in 1944. I tried to locate him in RAF records, but they could only find an airman of that rank who had won the Victoria Cross for his attack on a U-Boat in 1944. Although wounded, he pressed home his attack against fierce opposition from the surfaced

Flight Lieutenant Ian J. A. Cruickshanks
Wedding photograph

submarine and sank it. A photograph showed that they were not the same person. The Catalina pilot was tall and lean, my pilot had been short in stature.

I left it at that, but research has a habit of catching one unaware. I was reading a book by David J. Smith in the 1980s on the history of RAF Hawarden when it leapt out of the page at me. 'Two airmen from No. 48 MU were less lucky on the 8th June 1945 when their Halifax JP203 collided with a church steeple on approach to Rawcliffe near York. Flight Lieutenant I. J. A. Cruickshanks and Flight Sergeant V. H. Clare both lost their lives'. I thought of the pilot shaking me down from the gun turret and the searching look he gave me after signing my new flying log.

I found out that Flight Lieutenant Cruickshanks had been married and, by a stroke of good fortune, tracked down his widow since remarried. With the family's help and official records, this is his story.

He became a member of the RAFVR in September 1937. Two years later, on the outbreak of war he was mobilised. By June 1940 he was a pilot with No. 66 Squadron Coltishall ready for the Battle of Britain. He was in action several times including 20th August when his section was credited with one Messerschmitt 109 shot down and another unconfirmed. On 7th September he intercepted five large enemy formations, ending up with several large holes in his aircraft and cockpit. On 9th September his section shot down a Heinkel He 111, but on the 11th he was shot down himself, crash landing at Wye. He was flying again three days later.

Following these critical days he was posted to Baginton, near Coventry, where he tested new and repaired aircraft gaining an Air Efficiency Award. He then went on to RAF Hawarden in June 1943 carrying out similar work for No. 48 MU.

Two years later, on 8th June 1945, Flt/Lt Cruickshanks took off from Hawarden in battle-served Halifax JP203. With him was flight engineer F/Sgt V. H. Clare, who had served with No 77 squadron. He fought a fire on board Halifax LK710 on the 22nd of April 1944 but eventually was forced to give up and bail out of the aircraft. He evaded capture and returned to the UK and was later awarded the DFM. They set course for Rawcliffe, near York, where these old veterans were being scrapped. As they came in to land, just fifty feet above the runway and far too late, the Air Traffic Controller fired a Very pistol – he had seen that the undercarriage was not down.

The pilot opened up the throttles and pulled away, but at that critical moment the port outer engine failed. The drill in these circumstance would have been to land straight ahead but, unbelievably, there was a housing estate in line with the runway. They kept on flying just above the rooftops, but with the lack of power on one side the aircraft kept pulling to port and height could not be gained.

Fate now took a hand. The church steeple of St. Joseph's appeared in the line of flight. The Halifax was drawn to it like a moth to a candle flame. A wingtip struck the top of the steeple which made the difference between flying speed and stalling. In the dying seconds the pilot managed to avoid a large public house and dropped the huge aircraft in the back gardens between two rows of council houses in Kingsway where it broke up and burned out. Due to the skill of the pilot no-one on the ground was even injured, but both airmen lost their lives.

A few months previously Flt/Lt Cruickshanks had become a father. His son was to become a pilot in the RAF himself, a Squadron Leader flying such aircraft as Jaguars and Tornados at the forefront of Britain's

defence. His father would have been so proud of him. In 1996 the Yorkshire air museum provided a brass memorial plaque which was erected in St Joseph's. Members of the airmen's families attended including Air Commodore Cruickshanks, son of the pilot, the pilot's mother and two sisters of the flight engineer.

Memorial plaque to the crew of Halifax JP203 in St. Joseph's Church, Clifton (Fr. Jerry Twomey)

Grave of Flt/Lt Cruickshanks at Milverton Cemetery, Leamington Spa (Sam Wedge)

Chapter 1

The Downfall of a Dragonfly

West and north west of the slate quarries of Blaenau Ffestiniog lies an area of a rough and tumble of lesser known mountains, dominated by the 2265 ft Cnicht, in the shape of a perfect mountain. Trapped high in the little valleys are a dozen or more small lakes. One is known as Cwm y Foel. A dam was constructed there about 1908 to provide water for hydro electricity, providing power for the nearby Croesor quarry. Like most mountain regions in Wales it has a story. There is tendency for air pockets to occur in Cwm Croesor when the wind is strong. The turbulence sounds just like thunder coming from the gorge. A section of the cliff is known locally as Drws y Daran – the Door of Thunder.

In 1948, Sikorski in the USA, built a helicopter known as the S.51. This was built in Great Britain under licence by Westland Aircraft Limited and called the Dragonfly. Some were taken on by British European Airways for experimental services. With a leak causing problems at Cwm y Foel, urgent repairs were called for. On the 24th May 1949 one was offered to the dam company to see how it would fare transporting materials to the dam. This was registered as G-AKCU and piloted by Denys Bryon of Beckenham Kent. He was a former Bomber Command pilot. To transport the repair materials and up the mountain by hand was a daunting prospect which would take many weeks. At the end of the mountain track at Croesor Fawr farm some 880 pounds of cement was attached by nylon lines to the underside of the helicopter, which was

Westland Dragonfly G-AKCU. L-R Unknown, Pilot, Robert Arthur Williams, Griffith Williams, Harry Roberts of Groesor Fawr Farm, Iorwerth Ellis Williams. (Harold Morris via Pred Hughes)

The remains of Dragonfly G-AKCU (Harold Morris via Adrian Barrell)

flown down the valley to gain height, then climb to the dam wall at 1700 feet and discharge its load. This it achieved some 15 times. On the 16th lift as the h e l i c o p t e r reached the drop zone the engine cut out. The pilot hit the emergency switch which released the bags of cement all over the nearby rocks. Normally a helicopter could *windmill* safely to the ground, the rotors letting it d o w n . Unfortunately, the tail rotor hit the mountain side and the Dragonfly rolled down the steep slope turning over and over until it reached a level area below.

Griffith Griffiths, a quarryman waiting for the load rushed down to the wreck and wrenched open the door with a crowbar. Amazingly, the pilot walked away from the wreck and sat on a nearby rock. He had been warned by the local quarrymen about the Door of Thunder and to avoid flying past the cliff. He had ignored this advice so it is a matter of conjecture if the wind had any bearing on the crash in preventing a safe let down. The pilot was taken to hospital where it was found that he had no broken bones, surprisingly for those who had observed the Dragonfly bouncing down the mountain slopes.

Another Dragonfly, G-AJOV was flown in to complete the work which was accomplished without incident.

Sistership Dragonfly G-AJOV
(Harold Morris via Adrian Barrell)

Chapter 2

Twelve Miles

Flying Officer William (Billie) Auld, navigator

Flight Lieutenant Bert Grimshaw, navigator

At the time of this story, RAF Shawbury, just north east of Shrewsbury, was home to the Central Navigation School. Some exceptional navigators with operational experience were selected for a Specialist Navigation Course for special duties.

One of these was Flying Officer William (Billy) Auld, DFC. Prior to the war he had worked as a civil engineer in Nigeria. When World War II came about he volunteered for service in the RAF as a navigator. He eventually was posted to RAF Snaith, 51 squadron, 4 group on Lancasters. In the London Gazette of the 12th November 1943 he was awarded the Distinguished Flying Cross.

Another officer was Flight Lieutenant Bert Grimshaw D.F.C of Blackpool. He had been commissioned first of all in the Royal Engineers as a former civil engineer. When the RAF appealed for aircrew he volunteered and transferred to the RAF where he trained as a pilot. He then went to Coastal Command. At Wick he flew Hudsons of No 220 squadron carrying out shipping strikes off the Norwegian coast. Posted to Pembroke Dock he was soon flying the huge Sunderland flying boats of 228 squadron. On one occasion he and his crew fought off an attack by eight Junkers Ju 88 fighter bombers over the Bay of Biscay, shooting down two. Grimshaw was awarded the DFC for that action. In February 1944 his aircraft developed an engine fire after take off. He showed great coolness as he ditched the Sunderland in the open sea in the dark. The crew of a sister aircraft spotted the fire and picked up the crew.

On August 21st 1944 the two officers on the Navigation course met their staff pilot, Flight Sergeant Jack Firth and his wireless operator Flight Sergeant Ron Erickson, at Wellington MkX111, serial HZ699, and took off at 22:30 hours. The first leg of the flight carried them to Ballyquintin Point at the entrance to Strangford Lough, northern Ireland. Then a circle round and a heading for Strumble Head near Fishguard, then a third leg took them to Corsewall Point NNW Stranraer, then a turning point for a giddy crew for the Point of Ayr, and a course given to the pilot for the home run to Shawbury. The crew relaxed looking forward to a hot meal when suddenly a dark shape erupted in front of the Wellington. It struck the summit of a 1600ft mountain and broke up at 02:30 hours.

The senior boys of Bingley Grammar School were on a forestry camp at Rhos Pengwern farm near Llangollen along with their headmaster Mr Alan Smailes and two teachers. Mr Smailes was awoken at 03:15 am by the farmer, Mr F. Edwards. On leaving the

*Flight Sergeant Jack Firth,
pilot Wellington HZ699
(Jack Firth)*

*Flight Sergeant Ron Erickson,
wireless operator
(Jack Firth)*

bell tent he could see there were three fires on Y Foel, very bright and very red, burning fiercely. The farmer thought it might be a crashed aeroplane. Mr Smailes roused his two colleagues, Mr Dodd and Mr Laycock and eight senior boys and followed the farmer up the mountain. John Botterill was one of the boys called from his tent and made the climb to the mountain summit. 'I heard a moan nearby and, bending down, I saw an airman (F/Sgt Erickson) lying severely injured with a broken thigh and many head wounds. We covered him up so that he would not suffer from exposure and looked for other members of the crew. Then we found a chap who was past help. Later I heard someone groaning and saying *"Where am I?"* (F/Sgt Firth) I was crawling because of the explosions – perhaps machine gun ammo, and he was on his back with bloody froth coming from his mouth. I dragged him by the shoulders until he was clear of the dangers. I asked him the number in his crew. He said there was another one to find, who we found by the tail of the Wellington – his neck broken. He was wearing pyjamas under his flying suit.'

Mr Smailes realised that this was an isolated place, over three miles from Llangollen, but only one and a half miles from Glyn Ceiriog. He gave two of the boys a torch and, with the guidance of a farmhand, they ran

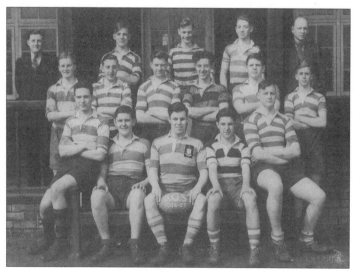

John Botterill. Bingley Grammar School rugby team captain.
(Alison McKinley – daughter)

Summit of Y Foel. Trig point top right. Possible damage due to crash. (Wendy Thomas)

to Glyn Ceiriog where they woke the local policeman who telephoned Llangollen and soon an ambulance was on its way. In the mean time the pilot was placed on a gate and carried down to the farm by five boys, the two teachers, and Mr Edwards.

On arrival Flight Sergeant Firth was covered in blankets and coats from the boys tent and placed in the ambulance which sped off for Wrexham hospital.

In the meantime a nurse came over the moor from Glyn Ceiriog with the help of the torch she immediately set about reviving Flight Sergeant Erickson, bandaging his head, and having the boys keep rubbing his feet and legs then others to make splints for his thighs then he was carried down to Rhos Pengwern farm where the RAF ambulance from Wrexham just arrived. After all this

Wellington in cloudland (Hope Roberts)

endeavour it is sad to relate Ron Erickson died on the way to hospital.

That afternoon an RAF wing commander came to the camp to investigate the crash. After taking statements and visiting the crash scene, he ventured that the Wellington was fully under control until the crash occurred. Instead of flying at a safe height of over 2000ft the pilot may have come lower to see if he could distinguish any land marks, the night being so dark. Had it descended 100ft less it would have cleared the mountain and then would have been over low ground to Shawbury. It was 12 miles off course.

The three airmen who did not survive the flight are buried in the CWGC cemetery at Blacon, near Chester. Bert Grimshaw married Sheila Mabel Inskip at Llandrindod Wells parish church in December 1943. Their son Robert Inskip Grimshaw was born on 11th October 1944, two months after his father lost his life.

Chapter 3

A Tale of Two Brothers

Sergeant Alf Hall, pilot of Blenheim L9039 (Bjorn Hall – nephew)

Alfred Ernest Hall was the older of two brothers who volunteered for the RAF at the start of World War II. After training he became a Sergeant pilot and joined No.13 Operational Training Unit at Bicester in 1940. On 8th April he took off on a cross country training flight in Bristol Blenheim Mk IV, serial L9039, code LD-Y. His crew of three were Observers Sgt F. Graham and Sgt A. C. Catton, and air gunner LAC G. H. Jones. In a formation of three aircraft they flew towards north Wales to cross the Irish Sea to Ronaldsway in the Isle of Man and return home via Hartland Point in Devon. However, on entering cloud, Sgt Hall banked his aircraft away from the others. As it exited the mist it flew into a shoulder of Carnedd Llewelyn (second highest mountain in Wales at 3,484 feet) known as Craig yr Ysfa (Itching Rock), with the loss of all the crew.

All these young men were precious to their families. In addition, Sgt Catton was reported to be a fine poet, a loss also to our heritage. In April 1990, the writer, as a Rowen school governor, took a party of senior pupils

Wreckage of Blenheim L9039 on Craig yr Ysfa (David Roberts)

from the school on the long trek to just below the crash site as a memory of the crew members fifty years on.

Jack W. G. Hall was the younger brother of Alfred. After his pilot training he was posted to RAF Wick in Caithness. This was about the nearest airfield to carry out attacks against enemy forces which had over run Norway. On 23rd December 1941 F/Sgt Hall and his crew of three took off for a patrol along the Norwegian coast in Lockheed Hudson MkV, AM678, code NR-U.

Reaching Bergen they flew south to Stavanger, the point at

Flt/Sgt Jack Hall at Stalag Luft VII in 1942 (Bjorn Hall)

which they would turn for Wick. The aircraft came out of the coastal mist to be faced with a large German convoy protected by a naval escort just a mile away on the shore side of the Feistein Rock. Hall reached down to operate the bomb-door lever. At that precise moment there was an explosion in the cockpit as they were hit by a shell from a German coastal flak battery at Vigdel. Co-pilot P/O H. D. C. Henderson took the full force of the shell which knocked out Hall.

On coming to, Hall found the aircraft flooding with water. Spotting his wireless operator, Sgt Stanley J. Price by the rear door he shouted 'Jump – she's going,' and leapt into the freezing waters. Luckily a fisherman, Sven Hellesto and his son Bjarne, had seen the plight of the Hudson crew and quickly launched a dinghy, then raced out some two hundred yards to the airmen. Here they pulled Hall and Price into the dinghy and then recovered the lifeless bodies of Henderson and Sgt Harold Hamer floating with their Mae-Wests on.

On reaching the shore a formidable reception committee of some 30-40 German soldiers was waiting for them.

Following a change into dry clothing and a few days in

Flight Sergeant Jack Hall & Sergeant S. J. Price being brought ashore. German soldiers are waiting.
(Tor Odemotland)

various cells, the airmen found themselves in Oslo. Jack Hall recalled 'At Gardemoen airport we were handed over to a Luftwaffe officer whose English was adequate enough to tell us that we were bound for Berlin. He, also, had been shot down near Sola – by his own German batteries, and was now grounded. There were two Junkers Ju52 three engined transports on the apron. As we boarded I noticed that the other aircraft was receiving a special party in dark uniforms, in the centre of which was an imposing figure with an impressive cloak with a heavy metal chain.'

We took off and headed for Denmark, landing at Alborg for refuelling. We learned before taking off again, that the other aircraft with the VIPs on board was overdue. When we landed at Copenhagen one of the Junkers crew invited us RAF airmen to lunch. We had a fine meal of goose with vegetables and ample supplies of lager. Then we were airborne again – destination Berlin. The cabin heating was poor. The cold and the plentiful supply of lager had its inevitable effect and I asked where the loo was. Alas, there wasn't one. The next hour was a fidget of crossed legs. At last we landed and I quickly stood beneath the fuselage and

Lockheed Hudsons of 220 Squadron (Simon W. Parry)

answered the call of nature. I can truthfully say that the first thing I did on reaching Berlin was to piss on it!'

Eventually, after interrogation at Dulag Luft at Oberausel near Frankfurt, Jack Hall was incarcerated at Stalag Luft III before being sent to Stalag 383 near Hohenfels. In the POW camps he was called Henry, after the well known dance band leader of the day – Henry Hall.

Henry was one of those internees who was either bored or felt it his bounden duty to escape. In July 1943 he crawled under a delivery lorry and concealed himself as the lorry left the camp. He was only spotted at the last moment at the outer gate by a suspicious sentry and sent back. In the following September he enterprisingly dug a hole in the sports field and waited until nightfall. Then he climbed out and was seen trying to crawl under the enclosing fence. Back again.

In November, Henry was in a work party planting potatoes in the fields. The prisoners were advised that this was the last day that they would be outside the wire getting some fresh air. One bit of luck came in the shape of the guard. It was Dopey. In no

Bjorn Hall with Mercury engine off the Blenheim
(Bjorn Hall)

time at all there were fifteen men left from twenty one who had marched to the field. Into the woods and towards the nearest railway station went Henry, Percy, Andrew Winton, and an Army Sergeant, Eddie Ramage. They came to the railway and climbed into a wagon during shunting operations. Soon the train was off and picking up more wagons at other stations. When it appeared that they would soon be in a large marshalling yard, they left the wagon and made their way through woods to a wide river. Finding a rowing boat the party got in and headed downstream until it looked as if they were near a populated area. A small bay was found to land and push the little boat on its way.

In the woods a meal was produced by starting a small fire and cooking some potatoes that they had kept. Then a reviving mug of tea. They rested in the night and were ready for the off at first light, estimating that they were about only fifteen miles from the Swiss border. Suddenly all their plans went haywire. A woodsman in green apparel appeared and indicated 'Hands Up' with his rifle. There was no safe way out of this and he took them to a nearby castle and locked them in a secure room. The caretaker and his wife were kinder people, and had a lovely ten year old daughter – Beate. When the escapees gave their word not to attempt escape, the party were moved up to a nicer room with bunk beds and washing facilities. Four bowls of soup followed along with sausage sandwiches.

To fill in the time, Andrew asked for some paper and pencils. When it was seen how good he was as an artist, the caretaker and his wife asked if he would draw Beate for them. After a few false starts Andrew eventually captured her on paper. Her parents and fellow escapees were greatly impressed with the likeness. Andrew said that it was the best drawing he had ever done.

A sergeant from Stalag 383 arrived to say that the train was not due until the next day. In the meantime he took them down to the river Isar and showed them the Blenheim battlefield of 1704.

Because the four had been model prisoners and kept their word at not attempting escape, the caretaker took them to a heavily locked door in the cellar. Here they were shown many superb paintings said to have been confiscated by Hermann Goering and were being kept for him. The next day the sergeant and two soldiers escorted the reluctant four back to Hohenfels, with a tearful farewell from the caretaker's wife and Beate. The camp commandant was not best pleased with the prisoners leaving the doubtful comforts of his camp, and sentenced each of them to thirty days in Straflager on bread and water.

Early in 1945 found many prisoners of war on long marches to the east, on which so many died of exposure. In one of the transit camps, Jack/Henry Hall made a good friend of Bernt Overegard, who was a teacher at Stavanger's oldest grammar

"Happiness" – Jack and Bitten set sail with Bernt Overegard (Michael Hall)

school. Jack was a survivor and was repatriated at the end of May 1945. Bernt invited him to Norway as life started to return to normal. Jack accepted and in 1946 was reunited with his rescuers, Sven and Bjarne Hellesto. Bernt also invited him to go sailing with him and his niece, Bitten. It was not long before Jack fell in love. Soon they married and had two sons, Bjorn and Michael. In 2003, Jack found a copy of 'No Landing Place' in a bookshop which told him for the first time which mountain had claimed his brother Alf, and what aircraft he was flying. When he made contact with the writer, he was given more details. Sadly, he died before being able to visit the site himself, but son Bjorn arrived in April 2005 for detailed directions and was able to find the wreckage of the Blenheim below Craig yr Ysfa. We have remained good friends ever since as all the photographs testify. It is so good to end a tale of tragedy and privation with a love story.

CWGC headstone of Pilot Officer H. D. C. Henderson at Sola (Michael Hall)

CWGC headstone of Flight Sergeant Harold Hamer at Sola (Michael Hall)

Chapter 4

Unlucky Marauder Crew

Airman to be, Kenneth W. Carty was born in Pasadena, Los Angeles, on 22nd June 1924, and educated at colleges in the area. He found employment with the Douglas Aircraft Company nearby at Long Beach, which produced such aircraft as the reliable transport known to us as the Dakota.

On 15th February 1943 Carty enlisted in the USAAF, volunteering for aircrew. Training under the blue skies of Kansas and Texas, he was awarded his wings and a commission on 15th April 1944. From then he eventually trained as a pilot of the chunky B26 Martin Marauder twin-engined medium bombers.

At Barksdale Field on 10th December 1944, 2nd Lt Carty came together with his crew and their shiny new B-26G Marauder, 44-68072. This powerful bomber was equipped with eleven 0.5 inch machine guns. In January came the time for departure from an airfield in Florida to Britain via the Southern Overseas Route. To Natal in Brazil, across the Atlantic to Dakar in west Africa, then Marrakesh, and onto St. Mawgan in Cornwall.

On 1st February 1945 the crew were briefed, along with fifteen other crews, for a flight to the large USAAF base at Burtonwood near Warrington. There were two changes to the crew for the next flight.

2nd Lt. Kenneth W. Carty, pilot.

2nd Lt. William N. Cardwell Jr, co-pilot.

1st Lt. Nolan B. Sowell, navigator.

Cpl Jack D. Arnold, engineer.

Cpl Rudolph M. Aquirre, radio operator.

Crew of B-26G Marauder 44-68072. L-R. 2nd Lt. K. W. Carty, pilot, 2nd Lt W. N. Cardwell, co-pilot, Lt Holmes (not on final leg) Cpl J. D. Arnold, engineer, Cpl R. M. Aqiurre, radio operator, Cpl Anderson (not on final leg). (David Roberts)

The briefing officer was at pains to to stress the height of the terrain in proximity to their route. Also, emphasis was placed on the winter weather to be expected. At higher altitudes the wind would be from 290 degrees, pushing them towards the mountains, at speeds of 40-50 mph. On the Beaufort Wind Scale this would reach force 9, a strong gale, which produces damage such as chimney pots and slates blown off.

The crews were advised to climb to 5,000 feet should they not have a visual sighting of their route, and fly on instruments. The aircraft were to fly to St. David's Head, then onto the USAAF airfield at Valley where a large change of direction would take them first to Woodvale just north of Liverpool. The sea route would keep them clear of the larger conurbations. A short flight would then see them safe at Burtonwood.

Lt Carty's aircraft took off at 1238 hours and set

2nd Lt Kenneth W Carty
(David Roberts)

Cpl Rudolph M Aquirre, left
(Rudi Lee – daughter)

course for St. David's Head. Of the other Marauders, 12 landed at Burtonwood, 2 at RAF airfields (possibly Woodvale), and one at Valley. There was no sign of Lt Carty's 44-68072. However, early in the afternoon a Crosville bus driver travelling at the bottom of the Llanberis Pass heard the sound of a low-flying aircraft, followed shortly afterwards by the sound of an explosion. In this quarrying area, explosions are common and he did not think to report it until the next morning. The RAF Llandwrog Mountain Rescue Team was called out and found the remains of

Y Garn with Cwm Cywion in dip beyond (Bob Lewis)

the Marauder and its crew on 3,104 feet Y Garn (the Cairn) which stands overlooking Llyn Ogwen.

A USAAF aircraft accident investigation team made their way to the scene. They found that the initial impact was at 3,000 feet and the aircraft disintegrated as it skidded over the top of the mountain with the main body falling into the high bowl of Cwm Cywion where it dropped 500 feet.

We may wonder why this aircraft came to grief when the others on the day got through. On landing at St. Mawgan, Lt Carty reported that the gyro compass had been oscillating by 10 degrees.

The compass was checked on the ground on four headings, but no fault could be found and the aircraft was passed as fit for service. Did some fault develop when the course alteration for Valley was made? The scar the Marauder made on Y Garn showed it had been flying a course of 040 degrees. Should we back track on this heading then we come to the area of St. David's Head. However, even if a faulty compass and a strong

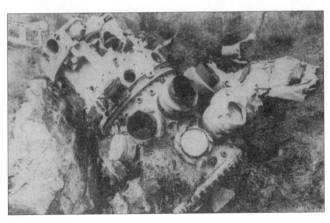

Double Wasp radial engine from the Marauder in Cwm Cywion
(Author)

westerly gale were to send them over the mountains of Snowdonia, the fate of the crew was sealed when it was decided to reduce height to 3,000 feet for the run to Valley. Otherwise the crew may well have come back to the sea at Llandudno.

One month later in Texas, Cpl Rudolph M Aquirre's wife gave birth to a baby girl, and named her Rudi in his memory. In 1999 Rudi visited Snowdonia and found the memorial to the Marauder crew in Llanberis Pass. She gave up an attempt to climb Y Garn, her mother had told her 'I have lost one member of my family to a mountain, do not make it two!'

Rudi made contact with the writer and we remain friends. A fine photograph of her father has resulted.

Memorial to Marauder crew at lay-by in Llanberis Pass (Author)

Chapter 5

Tomahawk V Elidir Fawr

Stephen Lovatt, a 51 year old classic car dealer, was quite used to flying around the Midlands area, but in July 2003 he arranged to meet another dealer, Ian Johnstone, at Caernarfon Airport. As this would be his first flight to the area he consulted the Chief Flying Instructor at Nottingham Airport, Richard Flanagan. He advised Lovatt to plan a fair weather route directly over Snowdonia, and an alternative along the coast, both via Crewe. On 10th July the pilot telephoned Caernarfon Airport at 0809 hours to obtain current weather information. The Airport does not have a meteorological observer, but the manager gave him a report on what conditions were, namely visibility of 8 to 9 kilometres, with a cloud overcast of about 1,500 feet. However, shortly after the call, the weather deteriorated to about 3 to 4 kilometres visibility, and a cloud base of about 1,000 feet ags.

The Piper Tomahawk G-BOCC left Tollerton airfield, near Nottingham at 0915 hours and flew to Crewe where the pilot chose the track of 270 degrees towards Caernarfon over the mountains of Snowdonia. The pilot contacted Liverpool Air Traffic Control (ATC) at 1009 advising that he was overhead at Wrexham and requested a Flight Information Service and permission to climb from 2,000 feet to 4,000 feet, which was granted. At 1039 Liverpool ATC advised him to contact RAF Valley for the rest of his flight. This was not done. This part of the flight has been gleaned from the GPS receiver of the aircraft and radar tracking records of the Tomahawk.

Just after leaving Liverpool ATC frequency, Lovatt descended from 4,000 feet to 3,000 feet about 5 nautical miles west of the Conwy valley, although there are a number of mountains above 3,000 feet. After another one and a half minutes, near Foel Goch, west of Capel Curig, the aircraft turned onto a northerly heading making a climb to 3,374 feet, and a minute later turned back onto a westerly track, climbing to 3,800 feet. Amazingly, it must have been close to overhead at the Ogwen Valley Mountain Rescue Organisation base near the eastern end of Llyn Ogwen. The aircraft then started to lose height towards 3,000 feet.

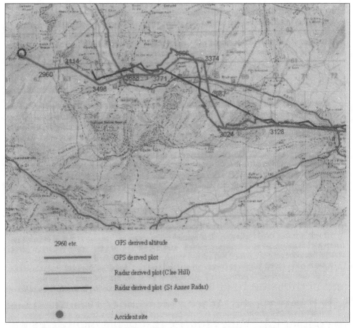

Radar and GPS plots of Tomahawk's flight showing changes in direction and height as it flew west towards Caernarfon
(courtesy AAIB)

Three hill walkers were at an altitude of 2,500 feet following a track 700 metres east of the summit of Elidir Fawr, which stands at 3,029 feet. At 1045 they heard an aircraft approaching, though they did not have a visual sighting with the hill fog and light rain. After the aircraft had passed the engine revs suddenly increased then ceased abruptly along with the sounds of a ground impact. The hikers telephoned the police with these observations. As the pilot had not filed a flight plan, it was not until Ian Johnstone turned up at Caernarfon Airport to meet Stephen Lovatt that the manager became aware of the non-appearance of the Tomahawk. He alerted the Rescue Coordination Centre. Their enquiries showed that a pilot had contacted Liverpool ATC en route to Caernarfon. Examination of radar recordings showed that an aircraft had disappeared in the general area of Llanberis. A Sea King search and rescue helicopter of 22 Squadron was scrambled.

Al Read was one member of the Ogwen Mountain Rescue Organisation alerted for a search. The Sea King picked up Al and two other members at Ogwen base and headed for Llanberis Pass where they flew slowly up and down below the 2,000 cloud base for an hour. Deciding that the crash site must be higher, the helicopter flew them round to Marchlyn Mawr, the upper storage lake of the pump storage hydro system used to produce electricity at times of peak demand. Al Read and the two other team members disembarked from the Sea King just under the cloud base. They split up, with Al going to the north side of the lake. Visibility was 20 to 40 metres in a heavy drizzle. It was slightly better in the gullies as he slowly gained height, curving round towards Elidir Fawr on very steep and rocky slopes. Then he came to Bwlch Brecan where he was able to join the path from Y Garn to the summit of Elidir Fawr.

Suddenly he spotted three shiny boulders. As he came closer he realised it was an aircraft. When he got to around fifty feet away he made a radio call that he had found the missing aircraft, knowing that he would be fully occupied shortly, and giving the location just east of the summit, and the registration number.

Then he observed a slight movement in the aircraft. He called this in and adding that he was going to assess the pilot. Al approached from the left and behind. It was clear that the aircraft had flown into the ground and slewed heavily. Opening the canopy he found the pilot covered in blood and blood coming from his mouth. Luckily, Al had been given first aid training and a week's medical course.

He asked the pilot if he could name the call sign of his 'plane, but the reply was that he could not recall

Piper Tomahawk G-BOCC on Elidir Fawr
(Richard Williams, courtesy Mark Brittain & Daily Post.)

anything. It was two hours since the Sea King had picked them up. At this point Al pulled the fire extinguisher out of the aircraft just in case of fire, though there was no smell of fuel.

Al got into the Tomahawk with difficulty and tried to examine the pilot, who was sitting leaning forward. Al moved him gently back, but Lovatt went forward again, apparently he had sustained some injuries to his spine when the seat was torn from its mountings on impact. Also his face had smashed into the control column causing the severe facial injuries that were so obvious. Al tried to place a collar round the neck, but the pilot would not tolerate it. At least he was able to check the pulse. At that moment another member of the team wandered into view, out of the mist and asked 'Do you want a hand?' Al had been on his own for at least twenty minutes.

Other team members then started to arrive. Clearly it was imperative to get the casualty off the mountain and to hospital as quickly as possible. The stretcher was put together and placed on the wing. Three team members got into the aircraft and lifted Lovatt out, rotating him onto the stretcher. After a quick assessment, the plan was made to find a safe route down the south-east flank of the mountain towards Llanberis. The pilot was tied in, though this compromised the airway which became very noisy. He was nearly unconscious. Visibility was down to 20-30 metres and they were bracing themselves against a strong wind. Down the team went, ropes in constant use, as they traversed the rocks and steep gradients. At one point they met Mark Tomlinson aka 'Tommo' from the Sea King, accompanied by a consultant surgeon. After a quick assessment, the advice was 'Keep going, get below the clouds'. They were forty minutes from the crash site. Then only another fifteen minutes and they were met below cloud by the Sea King. A race then to Yspytty Gwynedd and transfer to an ambulance and into the Resuscitation Unit, where Steven Lovatt was handed over to Pauline Cutting and her colleagues along with Al Read's written observations.

The pilot's injuries were severe, but he made a complete recovery in time, though could never recall the flight into Elidir Fawr.

Recovery of Tomahawk G-BOCC by Squirrel helicopter of Airbourne Soloutions. 11th July 2003. (John Ellis Roberts)

The Tomahawk was recovered by a helicopter being used by the Snowdonia National Park Authority and National Trust for path maintenance, to be taken for detailed inspection by the Air Accident Investigation Branch. No fault could be found with the Tomahawk. The Discussion in the report of the AAIB suggests that the pilot may have encountered a lowering cloud base and tried to stay beneath it. However, with only a telephone call to Caernarfon Airport to base his weather forecast on, it seems unlikely that he was aware of the poor weather over the mountain route he chose to fly on.

Elidir Fawr and Elidir Fach were the last mountains on the pilot's route. After those it was a clear run to Caernarfon airport.

Low

Chapter 6

The Goat Shed

Peter Rutter joined the RAF in 1937, became a pilot, and eventually was given a commission. Before and early in wartime he was flying the pencil shaped Armstrong Whitworth Whitley twin engined bombers with their crew of five. On 21st May 1940 Flying Officer Rutter was based at Dishforth in Yorkshire. At 2015 hours he took off in Whitley MkIV K9038 to attack railway marshalling yards at Krefeld, near Dusseldorf. Four hours later the crew reached their target and Sgt Nixon released the bomb load of 3,500 lbs. The rear gunner, Sgt A. C. McKenzie reported a direct hit and the pilot banked the Whitley in the opposite direction, taking the course given by Sgt Sampson, 2nd pilot and navigator.

Pilot Officer Peter Rutter – centre – at RAF Leconfield 1938 (P. Rutter)

They settled the aircraft at 11,000 feet with an airspeed of 185 mph. Later they entered a zone of bad weather, requiring Rutter to fly on instruments. The wireless operator, LAC White was finding it impossible to obtain a fix on their position, a pilot's nightmare. When the Whitley had reached eight hours in the air, they were fast approaching the limit of nine hours of fuel consumption. As luck had it, the pilot, eyes peering into the murk, spotted a broad hilltop poking just above the layer of mist. This had to be their only chance of a controlled landing. He offered his crew a chance to bail out, but there were no takers.

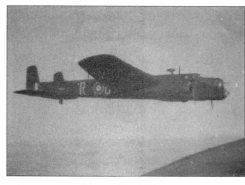

Armstrong Whitworth Whitley (Simon Parry)

It was moonlight and the landing lights illuminated the approach. Just in the nick of time power cables were highlighted and the aircraft was leap-frogged over them. Then they were on the ground, bumping along with the brakes hard on. They had made it and there were no injuries. When he had got his breath back, Peter Rutter got out and walked round the aircraft to see if there was any obvious damage. All seemed to be OK. As a matter of course he looked into the bomb bay.

Path of Whitley to Sheep Pens field (Jill Rutter)

There were two 500 lb bombs lodged in their racks! When the fog lifted a little at dawn, the pilot and another crew member went off for help. They were successful at an Elizabethan manor house – Golden Grove, which boasted a telephone. RAF Dishforth soon found out where their missing crew was, a field known as Sheep Pens between Llanasa and Gronant just inland from the holiday resort of Prestatyn. Later in the day the crew were delighted when their own maintenance engineer, Cpl Lawrence Elliott, arrived along with an armourer to defuse the bombs and a Rolls-Royce engineer who happened to be at the airfield.

While these experts checked the Whitley, the crew were taken to a pre-war Butlin's holiday camp taken over by the Army to have a good meal and a few hours rest. On returning, Cpl Elliott gave them the good news that their aircraft was undamaged. All that remained was to remove it from the field. Peter Rutter and Cpl Elliott paced the fields to check that they had a run of 1,000 yards for take off. With the removal of a hedge and filling in a ditch this would be possible – just.

The Army took on this task, but with the onset of dusk, this would have to wait until next day. When the day dawned the Rolls Royce engineer tuned the Merlin engines for extra boost. Cpl Elliott removed the machine guns and ammunition. Then enough fuel was fed into the tanks to get them to RAF Sealand, with a little to spare.

The electricity engineers shut down the supplies and removed the cables. At 1645 hours on 23rd May, F/O Rutter and his crew climbed aboard their aircraft which was taxied to the start of their run. Here the engines were run up and the brakes released. Over the undulating surface the bomber only slowly gathered speed until it eventually came over the brow of the last field and increased speed until suddenly it was airborne. There were cheers from the assembled villagers and schoolchildren who had witnessed this historic event. The bomber flew over the wide sands of the Dee estuary, past Neston where Nelson's love life, Lady Hamilton lived at one time, and refuelled at Sealand. By evening they were able to bring Whitley K9038 safely back to RAF Dishforth.

Had the hilltop not been spotted, the Whitley would have flown over the sea in a few minutes. The chances of surviving a night ditching were not good.

Peter Rutter's wife, Jill, could be said to be a Whitley nutter. She spent much time researching where any bits and pieces might be found. One loss she heard about was the forced landing of Whitley V BD 204 from Honeybourne in Wiltshire on 17th May 1943. It came down on mud flats at Point of Ayr at the tip of the Dee estuary following engine failure. All the crew survived, though the pilot, Sgt J. W. Clarke, was injured. As the aircraft was an obstruction, miners from the local colliery dragged it onto the dockside where much of it quietly melted away. In 1991 a large section of rear fuselage was found at Fynnongroew, a short distance from Point of Ayr. Peter Rutter came to see the section which was being used as a shelter for a nanny goat. Peter did a deal

The Goat Shed (Author)

with the farmer which saw the goat with a brand new warm shed and the goat shed section of Whitley transported to the Midland Air Museum at Baginton, Coventry. The hope was that one day it would fitted together with other recovered sections. Sadly, this now seems unlikely.

Jill Rutter also persuaded the writer to show her where a large sheet from Whitley BD232 had ended up in a hollow some distance from the slopes near Llyn Dulyn where it crashed on 26th September 1942 with the loss of all its crew. Jill, her two sons, and a friend trekked with the writer across a winter landscape to recover the section for it to join the goat shed at Baginton.

Recovery of part of Whitley BD232 near Llyn Dulyn (Jill Rutter)

Chapter 7

The Marl Farm Anson

RAF Mona in central Anglesey opened on 1st December 1942. With the demand for bomber crews increasing due to battle losses No.8 (O) AFU was formed here on 15th November 1943. Its Avro Ansons carried out many navigational flights over the western seaboard, day and night. The staff pilots and wireless operators took aboard trainee navigators, bomb aimers, and air gunners depending on which activity was required.

Flight Sergeant M. O. Samuels, RAFVR (Gwyneth Barratt – sister, via Gwyn Hughes)

On 15th February 1944 one such crew came together and climbed aboard Anson N5130, code 2-1. They were pilot F/Sgt M. O. Samuels, RAFVR, navigator P/O C. H. M. Folkard, RAFVR, wireless operator F/Sgt. T. M. Clothier, RNZAF, wireless operator Sgt. S. K. Yates RAFVR, and navigator J. M. Radecki, PAF (Polish Air Force).

The aircraft took off at 1505 hours and set course on

Sergeant T. M. Clothier, RNZAF (Jenny Gardner via Gwyn Hughes)

Sergeant S. K. Yates,
RAFVR (*Ken Yates via
Gwyn Hughes*)

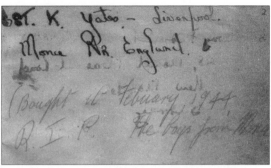

Sgt. S. K. Yates autograph (Hope Roberts)

the first leg towards Great Orme's Head, reaching the general area of Llandudno around 1530 hours. We were well used to the gentle sound of the Anson's Cheetah engines, many of which would fly over daily. This one was different.

Mike Sargent was seven years old at the time and his observations on that day have been riveted in his memory. 'We lived on Bryniau Road, West Shore, Llandudno. The day was calm, with a fairly clear blue sky. The road and general area was quiet. There was no noticeable aircraft noise. I was walking up the front path to the house when there was an extremely loud noise with no prior warning. The noise could be likened to a large vehicle skidding with its wheels locked. I turned around to see what was happening. I immediately noticed the Anson in question in the sky. From the position I was standing in, the aircraft appeared to be above the hill behind the Llandudno General Hospital.

For just a fraction of time the aircraft appeared to be stationary in the air, the fuselage was in a normal flying position with its wings horizontal. The aircraft was pointing towards me so there was a good frontal view. However, the wing sections outboard of the engines were missing. The engines and inboard sections were intact. The outboard sections which had been ripped off were reduced to quite small pieces, and were fluttering down around the fuselage. Then a fraction of a second later the nose dipped and the aircraft went vertically down behind the hill. The wing sections continued to float down to earth.'

Pilot Officer Humphrey Smith of 418 (Aberconwy) Squadron ATC was at his chicken farm on the hill at Llanrhos and had been drawn to the Anson's demise. 'It was diving and doing things an Anson should never be expected to do!'

They say that bad news travels fast. News of the crash reached my best pal John Meerwald and I in no time. We donned our ATC uniforms and cycled quickly to Marl Farm, Llandudno Junction. Here a steady stream of people followed a path to the corner of a field beyond a brick garden wall.

At the crash site all we could see was a heap of wreckage deep in the corner of a wet field. Thankfully, the bodies of the unfortunate crew had been removed and taken to RAF Mona. The other evidence in view was a half opened,

Anson N5130 crash site (author)

streamed out, parachute hanging from a tall tree in the wood bordering the field. One crew member had nearly made it, almost an impossibility in a diving aircraft.

The RAF Court of Inquiry into the accident concluded that an aileron had broken away and so the Anson suffered a complete loss of control as seen by those who observed the tragedy on that fateful day. Those who lost their lives were:

Flight Sergeant Melville Owen Samuels (23) buried at Heneglwys (St. Llwydian) churchyard, near RAF Mona, NE corner, Grave No.3.

Pilot Officer Charles Henry Melbourne Folkard (21), buried at Oulton (St. Michael) churchyard, Suffolk.

Sergeant Thomas Malcolm Clothier, (24) of Matamata, New Zealand, buried at Chester (Blacon Military cemetery), section A, Grave No. 945.

Sergeant Sylvester Kenneth Yates (20), buried at

Memorial in St Michaels and All Saints Llandudno Junction (Author)

Liverpool (Yew Tree) Roman Catholic cemetery, section 3c, Grave No. 33.

Jan Mikolaj (30) buried at Holyhead (St. Mary's) Roman Catholic cemetery, Grave No. 113.

They are not forgotten

The author is indebted to the Grwp Hanes Deganwy – History of Deganwy Group and web master, former colleague Gwyn Hughes for his detailed research and finding historic photographs.

On the fifteenth of February 2014, 70 years to the day from the crash a memorial service was held at St Michaels and All Saints Church, Llandudno Junction. Present were senior RAF officers and air cadets from number 418 (Aberconwy) squadron who provided a splendid guard of honour to the unveiling of a memorial to the Anson crew and also to one in the fine garden at the community centre. Five silver birch saplings have been planted, each one with the name of a crew member. During refreshments the writer was privileged to meet the sister of the pilot Flight Sergeant Samuels and relatives of Sergeant S. K. Yates.

F/Sgt Samuels sister with her son at the silver birch (Author)

Chapter 8

Waylaid by Wat's Dyke

Wat's Dyke appears to have been constructed to prevent raiders from the Welsh heartland from plundering the rich lands of Cheshire. It consisted of a simple broad earth bank and a deep ditch on its western side, built possibly between AD 400–600. The dyke ran some 40 miles from Maesbury Marsh south of Oswestry through such towns as Wrexham to Basingwerk Abbey close to the banks of the Dee estuary. Wat is a shadowy figure from the Dark Ages. What is certain is that the structure bearing his name was instrumental in stopping an aircraft skidding along the ground many centuries later during the Second World War.

Rootes Securities factory at Speke airport was in 1942 manufacturing Handley Page Halifax bombers in quantity. John Palmer was the chief test pilot at Speke, assisted by his chief flight engineer, a brilliant 23 year old with a calm temperament, most useful in his demanding job. In May 1942, a Halifax squadron reported serious vibration problems with its aircraft. Bomber Command requested that this be urgently investigated. On 20th May a test flight was set up from a new production line of MkV Halifaxes with Merlin engines. On board with John Palmer and his chief engineer was trainee engineer 40 year old Alfred Smith, Chief engineer for Rolls Royce engines (Derby), Chief engineer for Rotol Airscrews, and Speke's Flight Shed Superintendent.

Chief test pilot John Palmer & flight engineer with Halifax MkIII at Speke (John Palmer)

Test flight personnel 20th May 1942, L-R Mr Howlet, Rotol Airscrew Ltd, Mr Rimmer, Flight shed superintendant, John Palmer, Mr Goodall, Rolls-Royce engineer (John Palmer)

Halifax DG223 took off and flew down the corridor over the river Mersey, then across the Dee, to an area above Mold at 1,800 feet. John Palmer – 'After carrying out tests with alterations to throttle settings and pitch control, no vibrations were noticed. Then onto the second phase, feathering of each engine in turn, starting with the starboard outer, no resulting vibration so unfeathered. Then onto the starboard inner, commenced to feather but the aircraft swung to starboard since the outer engine failed to pick up. Suddenly, both port engines cut out. I suspected fuel starvation and requested the isolation cock to be checked. This was reported as being in the "ON" position. With no power we were rapidly losing height in an area of hills, ravines and boulders. There was no time to do anything but put her down, wheels up. All on board, saving the flight engineer, were sent quickly to crash positions. Then, under the port wing appeared a small grass field. We were down to 200 feet. I turned in; the airspeed with no drag from the undercarriage or flaps was 120 mph. To help reduce the forward speed I

Halifax went through hedge, across far field, and was stopped by tree-topped Wat's Dyke
(author, courtesy Chris Maddock)

put the nose down through a thick hedge, taking the nose section out. We sped across the field on our belly towards the far side. By a miracle there was a grass bank about four feet high, slightly sloping and surmounted by trees. (Wat's Dyke) This brought us to an abrupt halt. The only injury was a small cut to my forehead. To my dismay the trainee engineer was killed when we went through the hedge. I had no idea he had gone into the bomb-aimer's position in the nose.'

Alfred Smith (Mrs J. M. Schonnberg – niece)

John Palmer looked about for any roads or habitations in this remote area. Eventually he found a lone farmhouse after wading through a stream. The owner thought he was a German! It took some time to convince him otherwise. From there the pilot was able to telephone worried staff at Speke with news of the accident. Later, the assistant test pilot flew over and reported their position back to Speke. An Air Ministry official arrived at 7.0. pm. The body of Alfred Smith was taken to farm buildings and a Home Guard detachment detailed to guard the aircraft. At last John Palmer was transported back to Speke, just stopping once in a blacked out village for a large tot of whisky. He arrived back at 11.30 pm, absolutely exhausted. It is safe to say that in the hands of John Palmer, the survivors could not have fared better. Experience and a cool head saved them.

An investigation showed that the fuel cock was incorrectly assembled. When indicating 'ON', it was 'OFF', and vice versa.

In spite of extensive research it has not been possible to find where Alfred Smith was buried.

The Halifax was recovered and repaired within a month. It was allotted to number 158 Sqn, then based at East Moor at that time. On 6th December 1942 DG223 coded NP-Q it took off from Rufforth at 1655 hrs for an operation to Mannheim but within minutes of clearing the airfield, the pilot called base to say he was returning with a jammed undercarriage. The Halifax failed to land after its first approach and crashed at 1728 hrs while going round again. It came down near Bilborough just off the main Leeds to York road.

Crew:

Pilot. Sgt J. Bartlett RNZAF injured
Flt Eng Sgt J. Thorogood injured
Nav Sgt L. E. W. Jackson killed
Bomb aimer Sgt I. U. McLauchlan injured
W/Op Sgt J. Battey injured
MUP Gunner Sgt P. T. Wallis killed
Rear Gunner Sgt B. A. Miller injured

By the time it crashed DG223 had already carried out eight previous bombing operations with the squadron.

WET

Chapter 9

Maid of Harlech

Harlech Castle, built for Edward 1st towards the end of the thirteenth century and Owain Glyndŵr's principal fortress during his national revolt at the begining of the 15th century, stands on a rocky prominence overlooking Cardigan Bay. Many centuries later in September 1942, visitors to its lofty walls would have observed a remarkable incident taking place seawards.

Robert Frederick Elliott was born in September 1918 in Rich Square, North Carolina. From his teenage years he was interested in aviation. Later, while in the regular Army, he enlisted as an aviation cadet in July 1940. On 14th March 1941 he was awarded his pilot's wings and given a commission in the USAAF. Following a period as a flying instructor in Arizona he joined the 49th Fighter Squadron, part of the 14th Fighter Group. Their Lockheed Lightning twin-boomed fighters were flown over via Canada,

P-38 Lightning at Atcham, as other aircraft circle (Sherril D Huff)

Greenland, and Iceland to Scotland and onto Atcham in Shropshire.

Fork-tailed devil. Symbol of 49th Fighter Squadron, USAAF. (Sherril D Huff ex-49th F.S.)

The rest of the pilots and ground support arrived by ship in Liverpool on 18th August 1942 and were transported hence to Atcham.

Soon the squadron was in action taking part in fighter sweeps, code named 'Wildflower', along the Dutch and Belgian coasts during September. Towards the end of the month the 49th Sqn was sent to RAF Llanbedr on the west Wales coast for gunnery practice. At 1400 hours on 27th September, Lt Elliott took off in P-38F Lightning 41-7677 as a target tower for the rest of the squadron. This involved towing a highly visible yellow drogue or sleeve some distance behind the aircraft. Elliott took off using the reserve fuel tanks, but did not switch to the main tanks after fifteen minutes. As a result the port engine closed down due to fuel starvation. The pilot dropped the target drogue over the airfield and flew out over the Irish Sea to turn and make his landing approach. At this point, the starboard engine shut down so an attempt was made to glide to the sandy beach, only to ditch in about two feet of water. Lt Elliott was uninjured, but was disciplined for not observing the Flight Operating Instructions. The engineering

2nd Lt Robert F. Elliott (Robert M. Elliott)

officer recommended that the P-38 be salvaged.

While Field Marshal Rommel was retreating through Libya pursued by the British Eighth Army commanded by General Montgomery, a second front was opened with the invasion of French North Africa in Algeria: Operation Torch. American troops landed on 8th November 1942, supported by naval forces. They were followed next day by British troops. On 11th November, Casablanca in Morocco, so well known later by the film of the same name starring Humphrey Bogart, Ingrid Bergman and Claude Raines, surrendered.

The 49th Fighter Squadron and the rest of the 14th Fighter Group flew to Algeria, in mid-November, moving to Maison Blanche on the 18th. This was a hazardous base to be in. On the night of 20th November an enemy bombing raid had started fires amongst several parked aircraft. Flying Officer Hugh G. S. Wyrill DFC was running to his Beaufighter where his radar operator Sergeant J. Willins was waiting to move the aircraft away from the flames. A bomb exploded ten yards away killing the pilot instantly. He is buried in El Alia Cemetery, Algiers. (see 'Fallen Eagles').

The 49th FS moved base on 22nd November further east to Youks-les-Baines, close to the Tunisian border. On 27th November, Lt Elliott and Lt Arthur Cole of the 48th FS, took off to carry out attacks against enemy forces. Lt Elliott's aircraft was hit, but still flying. Lt Cole landed on a dry lake bed with the intention of flying them both off at daybreak. Night was imminent. Unfortunately Lt Cole's aircraft suffered an undercarriage collapse on the rough surface. Lt Elliott landed by him with wheels up. The next morning they set their aircraft on fire and returned to base with the help of friendly Arabs.

On 5th December at 1220 hours, six P-38 Lightnings took off to escort nine A-20 Douglas Havoc twin-engined bombers

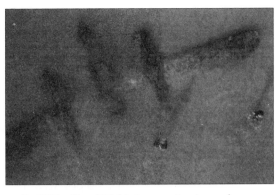

P-38F Lockheed Lightning 41-7677 in sands near Harlech (copyright TIGHAR via Matt Rimmer)

which bombed Bizerte airfield on the north coast of Tunisia. Lt Elliott was one of the escort. Returning from the targets, the Lightnings were attacked by a superior force of around 10-15 Messerschmit Me 109's. Of the enemy force, two were claimed shot down, plus two probables and two damaged. The price however was high. Lt Carlton was the only pilot to fly back to base. Both Lt Earnhart and Lt Gustke crash landed in the desert and made their way back to base.

Capt H. F. Lewis and Lt John P. Stief were killed in action. No trace of Lt Robert F. Elliott or his aircraft was ever found. With global warming his aircraft may appear as the lakes in the area dry out in years to come.

The P-38 41-7677 near Harlech had not been salvaged – just forgotten as the sands of time and Harlech beach washed over the wreck and buried it. On 31st July 2007 a local resident and his family were enjoying a day on the beach when he discovered the wreckage of a twin-engined aircraft in shallow water. A north Wales newspaper printed the photograph. Matt Rimmer, an aviation historian who lives locally, recognised the type of aircraft in the photograph and contacted The International Group For Historic Aircraft Recovery (TIGHAR) in the USA. A party from this organisation, including the founder Ric Gillespie, visited the site in October 2007 to see the Lightning at first hand. They photographed the aircraft with the aid of a kite held camera, producing an unforgettable image.

The problem which now remains is recovering the Lightning, a very expensive task, without further damage, and transporting it to a museum which can house it. Until then the sands have reclaimed the P-38, keeping her safe from possible vandals and from the sea.

Chapter 10

Disaster at Rhosneigr

One of the early units to be based at RAF Valley in Anglesey was No.4 Air Observers School (AOS). On 28th August 1941 news came through that a convoy off Holyhead was being attacked by enemy bombers. In spite of appalling weather, Blackburn Botha L6417 took off at 1130 hours to engage the hostile force. However, as soon as the aircraft was airborne, witnesses observed the Botha to lose power and ditch in the angry seas. The crew of three were Polish pilot Sgt, K. S. Rosevits, LAC T. A. Dickson, LAC F. C. Procter.

The crew quickly exited the Botha, but two were washed away and soon drowned. The pilot managed to claw his way onto the top of the fuselage. He was seen from the shore waving his arms to attract attention, then beating them around him to keep warm. His plight was seen by those ashore including two seventeen year old friends on holiday, Derrick Hubert Baynham of Walton on Thames, and John Stewart Wood of Chester. They launched a dinghy from the beach and rowed out to the plane against a vicious headwind and daunting waves.

The journey took them three quarters of an hour to reach the stricken aircraft, only for the dinghy to capsize as a huge wave hit it close to the Botha. Baynham called to the pilot to join them at the upturned boat, but he was reluctant. Baynham then swam round to the tail and climbed aboard from there.

He just reached the pilot when a mountainous wave washed them both off. The teenager swam after the airman with an oar with which they made it back to the dinghy. The boiling sea kept turning the boat over and over, and the pilot was steadily weakening.

In the meantime other would be rescuers were busy, dragging a whaler into the sea. The local Police Constable, C. G. Arthur along with seaman Arthur Owen, with soldiers and civilians, started rowing into the storm. Within minutes the boat was swamped and the makeshift crew thrown into the water. Those on the shore immediately formed a human chain stretching out into the bay in an effort to save them. One soldier on the beach swam out to where survivors were clinging to an oar some fifty yards away and brought them back, thus saving their lives. Then two other boats were launched, having been brought by lorry from Holyhead. Both capsized in the atrocious seas, the like of which had never been seen at Rhosneigr. RAF aircraft flew overhead attempting to drop lifebelts for those in peril.

Teenagers Baynham and Wood managed to get the exhausted pilot to a post sticking out of the waves, but he could not hold on and

Memorial to those who lost their lives at Rhosneigr 28th August 1941 (author)

was taken by the sea. They were fortunate when waves washed them into the arms of the human chain and they were brought safely to the shore. They were placed in an ambulance which sped them to Valley Hospital. The ambulance suffered two accidents on the way.

The gallant Constable C. G. Arthur and Merchant Seaman Arthur J. Owen were drowned along with soldiers and civilians. Including the Botha crew there were fourteen lost to the sea that day.

G. Arthur. D. W. Bannister. R. Eaton. L. A. Ford. E. Jones. A. W. Moger. A. J. Owen. R. K. Simons. C. H. Thorton. P. T. Whysall. S. Wilkins.

By a terrible quirk of fate the only vessel capable of operating in these seas, the Holyhead lifeboat, was out of action – in the shipyard for an overhaul. The lifeboat from Porthdinllaen on the north west of the Lleyn peninsular arrived at 1430 hours, three hours after the Botha ditched.

Derrick Baynham and John Wood were awarded the George Medal for their rescue attempt and the Silver Medal for gallantry from the Royal Lifeboat National Institution, also signed silver cigarette cases from General Wlalyslaw

John Stewart Wood & Derrick Hubert Baynham at Buckingham Pallace after the award of George medals by the King
(Sarah Robinson, Wood's daughter)

Sikorski, Commander in Chief, Polish Forces. The RNLI also awarded bronze medals to eleven other would be rescuers, seven of them posthumously.

As a sixteen year old, Baynham was at St. George's College, Weybridge in June 1940. When news of the evacuation at Dunkirk came through, he accompanied his bank manager in the latter's 30 foot motor yacht to Dunkirk and succeeded in evacuating three boat loads of troops. In the last rescue they were so overloaded that the soldiers were taken on board a destroyer before Baynham and his bank manager returned safely to Dover. Derrick Baynham was no stranger to adventure, which continued as his turn came to be called up for military duty in 1942. He was accepted into the Royal Corps of Signals where he volunteered for special duties. He was trained in sabotage and other hair-raising activities before instruction at the SOE signals school.

In the autumn of 1942 he and a female SOE radio operator were flown by RAF Lysander to a landing strip in the unoccupied zone of France south of the river Loire. He called her Angel, though this was not her SOE name. On landing, the agent they were supposed to meet was not in evidence, He had been arrested. Plan B was to make contact with the SOE circuit centred on Limoges, code named 'Ventriloquist'. Although they had help from French inhabitants in the area, they were unable to make contact with operatives in the circuit. The pair only narrowly escaped capture by the Vichy government's security police, the Milice.

After assessing the reliability of a nearby farmer, Baynham sent Angel to him with a message while he prepared to contact SOE HQ in London. While he was setting up his radio aerial in a disused pigsty, he turned round to find a Milice officer covering him with a revolver. At this moment a shot rang out and the officer fell at his feet. Angel had returned from the farmer, quickly assessed the situation, and fired the fatal shot. Moments later a second Milice officer came to investigate what was going on. He too was shot. Their bodies were placed in the Milice van which was tipped off the road down a steep slope into the woods below.

After hiding their radios in a ruined farm, the two agents left for Perigueux. As they had been unable to make contact with the local SOE network, they were in obvious danger. London control ordered them to proceed northwards and await pick up at another landing strip. However, Angel developed a serious chest infection. Baynham took her to a convent for treatment where she remained until France was liberated. Baynham found the landing strip and was flown home.

On his return Derrick Baynham was commissioned in the Royal Signals, then served with the Guards Armoured Division as it fought its way from Normandy to the Baltic. He was wounded by grenade fragments in his face and taken prisoner by the enemy. He escaped to his own lines and was mentioned in dispatches. Baynham stayed in the Army post-war with many appointments and postings from Palestine to Singapore. Promotions came, achieving the rank of Brigadier and ending his career as Chief Signals Officer, UK Land Forces. At this time he was appointed ADC to the Queen. He retired from the Army in 1979 and died on May 16th 2006.

John Stewart Wood eventually moved back to Rhosneigr and worked for a firm in Bangor. He died in 2014.

Chapter 11

Saved by the Navy

Situated on a peninsular south-west of Caernarfon, RAF Llandwrog was always going to suffer some take-offs and landings which would end in the sea. Some would take place a little further away.

Staff pilot Flying Officer Jack Stevenson took off on 16th October 1944 in Anson DJ621 to fly a navigational exercise around the Irish Sea. His crew consisted of navigator Wallace Kyd, RAAF, a bomb aimer, and a wireless operator. The first leg of the flight was south to Fishguard, flown at a height of 7,000 feet. The planned next leg was north to the Calf of Man, a small island off the south west tip of the Isle of Man. Here was situated an infra-red target for the bomb aimer to practice his skills.

However, fate took a hand instead. The propeller of the port engine suddenly took off, deciding to go it alone, and shot ahead of them. The pilot shut the engine down. As he did so, the engine cowling blew off, followed by the engine cylinders. Stevenson thought he might have to land in Eire, but he had planned to marry on 28th October. Now, close to 5,000 feet he quickly requested a QDM, or course to steer for Llandwrog. However, the Anson did not like flying on one engine, and was gradually losing height. Soon the pilot had to make a MAYDAY call and prepare to ditch.

Like an answer to a prayer, an aircraft carrier appeared steaming south towards them when they had dropped to 1,500 feet. The wireless operator signalled

Anson DJ621 ditched, with a dinghy and rescue whaler watched over by patrolling Anson (Wallace Kyd, copyright MOD)

the carrier with a request to land alongside. This was granted and Stevenson ditched slightly ahead and on the lee side. The operation went according to plan with a copybook landing.

Wallace Kyd was in the passageway when the bomb doors flew open and he was washed to the back of the Anson. Whilst being washed back and forth by the sea water he took charge of getting the dinghy out of the aircraft. The rest of the crew stepped into it without getting a foot wet. A longboat was launched from the carrier, took the dinghy in tow and returned to the ship. The carrier was

HMS Argus takes on rescued Anson crew via their whaler (Wallace Kyd, copyright MOD)

HMS Argus. Having served its time, it was being taken to a scrapyard on the Thames. The rescue launch then arrived from Fort Belan, close to Llandwrog. to collect the crew. The captain of the Argus, having got his vessel under way, would not stop his ship again.

The Anson crew then spent several relaxing days cruising with the Royal Navy. Anson DJ621 did not want to sink. It could not be left as a hazard to shipping, so the carrier gunners dispatched it by gunfire, watched by its melancholy former aircrew. Wallace Kyd, later Warrant Officer was singled out for a commendation for his actions by the Station Commander.

Anson navigator Wallace Kyd, RAAF

Anson pilot P/O Jack Stevenson and wife Monica – right (Monica Stevenson)

Chapter 12

The Lonely Sea and the Sky

John Spiers was a former RAF pilot and later a builder who used his French built Jodel DR1050, registration G-BAMW, to travel between homes in the Isle of Man and one in Kent. On August 2nd 1980 he placed his family, wife Carol, daughter 3 year old Leoni, and 3 month old baby Tristan in the Jodel at Ronaldsway airport. He then booked out with the Air Traffic Control (ATC) at 1000 hours, but did not obtain a route weather forecast or file a flight plan, His intention was to fly to Headcorn airfield in Kent making landfall at Point of Ayr at the entrance to the Dee estuary.

As the pilot left Ronaldsway controlled airspace he informed Liverpool ATC that he was cruising at 1,500 feet with an estimated time of arrival (ETA) of 1045 at Point of Ayr. At 1048 hours Liverpool ATC asked the pilot if he had the Point of Ayr in sight. The pilot's reply was 'No – I think I am probably a bit further west'. A prophetic statement.

At 1039 hours Spiers called the ATC to say that he was losing power, but did not give a MAYDAY call. At 1040 hours he reported that he had engine failure and gave an estimated position of between 3 – 5 miles from the coast. Conditions were misty but he said that he could see a small island to his right. At 1043 the pilot announced that he was ditching close to a fishing boat.

The emergency services were alerted and concentrated at first around Hilbre Island in the Dee estuary just off the Wirral peninsula. No wreckage or occupants were found, so the search was extended to include the River Dee and the north Wales coastline, plus the Jodel's track from the Isle of Man radar position. Helicopters joined in the search along with lifeboats from Rhyl, Flint, West Kirby and Hoylake. Coastguards and police made shoreline searches and shipping was alerted.

In fact the Jodel had ditched and inverted some five and a half miles from Great Orme's Head, much further west than the searches were being organised. With the cockpit cover being torn off, Carol Spiers had the baby torn from her arms. She was a non-swimmer and nearly drowned until she surfaced and managed to cling onto a wing. In the meantime her husband had made his way with great difficulty to the back seats to attempt to rescue Leoni. This was to no avail and they both drowned. Carol Spiers, at least found that the wrecked aircraft was still floating and clung to a wing for hours and hours. Just when she had nearly given up hope of being rescued, the crew of a Dutch coaster the Irene S, spotted the wreckage at 2054 hours and brought the survivor aboard. It would soon be dusk. A rescue helicopter from 22 Sqn RAF Valley was soon on the scene and winched her aboard Pilot Flight Lieutenant 'Taff' Evans flew swiftly to the C&A Hospital at Bangor while Air Loadmaster Bob Danes wrapped Mrs Spiers up in blankets and turned on the heating.

The Llandudno lifeboat was despatched to the Irene S to take the Jodel in tow. This was achieved with difficulty because of now choppy sea conditions. The tail came off and the speed had to be reduced to around 2 mph until they reached north shore,

*In the early
morning light,
Jodel G-BAMW is
brought ashore at
Llandudno's
north shore
(Glyn Davies)*

*Jodel G-BAMW on Llandudno's north shore
promenade 3rd August 1980 (Glyn Davies)*

Llandudno towards dawn. Here, the wreckage was brought ashore with the help of local people and holiday makers about.

The Air Accident inspectors eventually deduced that the engine failure was due to the failure of the exhaust manifold gasket. As this was inside the engine cowling the gases were re-ingested by the carburettor resulting in engine failure. The inspectors also noted that none of the occupants of the aircraft had been wearing lifebelts. All bodies had been recovered.

Carol Ann Spiers made a full recovery and later married Bob Danes. When she was just thirteen she made contact with the artist L. S. Lowry (no relation). He became a frequent visitor at the family home. When he died in 1976 he left her a substantial cash sum and paintings and drawings of his worth an estimated £500,000. For some years the Salford City Council had worked to rejuvenate an old pier – Pier 8 on Salford Quay. This was achieved in 2000. A theatre and gallery complex was built and named the Lowry Centre in honour of the artist. It was opened on October 12th 2000 by HM the Queen.

Chapter 13

Anson Dive off Wallog

Wales Coast Path runs north from Aberystwyth and past the hamlet of Wallog some three miles away. At low and spring tides looking out to sea from there, a causeway can be seen, looking for all the world if it continues to Ireland. Inevitably, there are legends associated with the causeway, which is known as Sarn Cynfelyn. One is that it was part of Cantre'r Gwaelod – The Lowland Hundred – a rich land swallowed by the sea in a terrible storm. In fact it, and a few others like it along this coast, are moraines left by glaciers during the last ice age. Just half a mile off shore near the causeway probably lie the engines and other parts of a wartime aircraft.

Avro Anson N5281 was based at No6 Air Observers School (AOS) at RAF Staverton. On 6th November 1942, while attached to RAF Aberporth, it took off on a navigational training flight northwards. After passing Aberystwyth, the pilot for some reason, possibly wishing to relieve himself, handed the controls over to the staff observer, Sgt W. Hall. He was not a trained pilot, and suddenly the Anson dived into the sea at 1605 hours.

The crew of a nearby fishing boat had observed events and quickly made their way to the scene, where three airmen were lifted from the water, one alive and two dead. The Aberystwyth lifeboat searched the area, but no trace of the remaining two airmen could be found. The Barmouth lifeboat was launched, but was recalled after radio contact with the other vessel. Eventually the bodies of the other two airmen were washed up for them to have a known resting place.

Sarn Cynfelin stretches out into Cardigan Bay off Wallog. Anson N5281 came down in sea around mid left of photograph. (Janet Baxter)

The crew of Anson N5281 were:
   Sgt. Claude E. P. Evans, pilot Buried at Towyn.
   Sgt. W. Hall, staff observer.
   LAC Vincent Henry Wright, trainee navigator.
   LAC F. A. Zinke, trainee navigator.
   LAC T. Booth, trainee navigator. Injured, but the only survivor.

In the meantime, Westland Lysander V9444 of 276 Sqn D flight search and rescue had taken off from RAF Fairwood Common in South West Wales to assist in the search for survivors.

However, the weather rapidly deteriorated and the aircraft was recalled by the flight controller. He was concerned when the Lysander did not make an appearance on time. In fact an electrical storm had damaged the compass and the pilot, Flying Officer John Anthony Dobson, became lost.

Not only this, but he realised that he was using a rich mixture of petrol to the engine and so was running out of fuel. He spotted the cliffs of Penbrokeshire coast, came closer and the decided not to climb above them because of entering cloud and by now it was dark. He decided to ditch about 50 yards from the

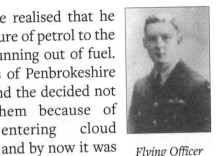

Flying Officer J. A. Dobson (Steve Jones)

shore off Abereiddy, and advised his gunner Sgt Alfred George Davis to prepare for this. On ditching, Dobson managed to climb into the dinghy, but Davis was drowned adding to the tragic list for the day. Six months earlier he had bailed out from a Defiant of 125 Sqn.

Sgt A. G. Davis (Steve Jones)

Lysander site off Abereiddy (Steve Jones)

Flying Officer Dobson landed near Ogof Morlonaid on the north eastern side of St. David's Head and made his way to the isolated village Treledydd Fawr where he found a hot bath and food. Sgt Davis' body was never found and he is remembered on the Runnymede memorial to missing airman.

Chapter 14

Third in Line

In June 1942 RAF Atcham near Shrewsbury became USAAF Station F342, the base for the 495th Fighter Training Squadron. Initially Lockheed P-38 Lightnings were based here, and later the chunky Republic P-47 Thunderbolts, the heaviest fighter of World War II, with its Pratt & Whitney R-2800 Double Wasp engine.

At 1545 hours on 23rd July 1944 Lt Willis W. Bryant took off and flew to the west on a 5A mission (cross country under 10,000 feet), with Lt Kenneth K. Cobb as his wing man. Ten minutes later he noticed that two other aircraft had latched onto them. They were the aircraft of Lt Benjamin A. Brew followed by that of Lt Frank J. Bates.

After some forty minutes the formation reached Cardigan Bay at Tywyn where they altered course northwards and decreased altitude to 500 feet. Lt Bryant then decided to cut across the Llŷn peninsula from Pwllheli to Nefyn, and was followed by the three other pilots. Shortly after reaching the sea again Lt Bryant spotted a ship a mile off shore and swooped across its bows, executing a roll, then climbed to 1,200 feet. He was followed by Lt Cobb who carried out the same manoeuvre.

Third in line, Lt Brew attempted to copy them, executing a roll, but stalled his aircraft at about 700 feet and plummeted into he sea.

Lt Bates, last in the line, observed the accident but, because his radio was faulty, could not contact the leader. He later said 'I buzzed the spot he hit and there was no part of his ship on top of the water' neither was there any sign of the pilot. Lt Bates did not carry out any rolls or other aerobatics, but caught up with Lts Bryant and Cobb to land back at Atcham at 1715 hours where the others learned of the loss of Lt Brew.

Searches in the area off Nefyn only found an oil slick. Lt Benjamin A. Brew is listed on the Wall of the Missing at Madingley US Cemetery, near Cambridge.

Lt Benjamin Brew
(David Von Rinteln, nephew)

Lt Benjamin Brew
(David Von Rinteln, nephew)

Republic P47 Thunderbolt 16234 at Atcham
(David Von Rinteln)

Chapter 15

Lost

The Short Stirling was the first of our four engined heavy bombers to see service with the RAF, in August 1940. One of the squadrons operating this type was No. 7 based at RAF Oakington. On 26th March 1942, three of their Stirlings joined a force of twenty seven aircraft to bomb the naval installations at St. Nazaire facing the Bay of Biscay. One of the three taking off at 1911 hours was N6074, code MG-G. Another eight aircraft of 7 Sqn were destined to join a force to attack Essen.

On the return flight MG-G flew into thick cloud. Radio fixes were obtained too late to be of use. Four of the crew were given orders to bale out, Sgt Bentham – wireless operator, Sgt Fenton – flight engineer, Sgt Williams – front airgunner, and Sgt Hudson – rear airgunner. They all landed safely. Those remaining were 1st pilot Squadron Leader H. L. Legh–Smith, 2nd pilot Sgt Bird, and observer Sgt Cooper. By now the decision was taken to ditch the aircraft as it was running out of fuel. The Stirling was ditched successfully in Cardigan Bay at 0143 hours. The three crew members made a safe exit into the dinghy and rowed to the shore. Had they but known it, they were just six miles south-west of RAF Llanbedr on the coast south of Harlech. With its long runway it could easily have accommodated the Stirling.

Two lifeboats had been launched, the 'Lawrence Arden' of Barmouth, and the Pwllheli lifeboat. They found the Stirling still floating with its hatches open.

The following day it was towed to Abersoch for salvaging.

How good it is to complete the main chapters of this work with an all survivor story.

Short Stirling N6074, code G-MG, at RAF Oakington (David Roberts)

PHOTOFILE & SHORT STORIES

1. The Sea King

The Sea King has now been replaced by red and white Sikorsky helicopters operated by Bristow from Caernarfon airport. The writer is pleased to pay a tribute to the Sea Kings of 22 Sqn, 'C' Flight and to their crews. In October 2010 I was invited with grandson Geoffrey Wedge, a documentary photographer, to the search and rescue centre at RAF Valley. The invitation came from Squadron Leader 'Spike' Wright and we were shown round the operations centre and a mighty Sea King by Flight Sergeant Nick Swannick. How all that weight including crew, stretchers, heavy bags of medical supplies, and a possible mountain rescue team was lifted off the ground is one of the wonders of aeronautical science.

The author dwarfed by Sea King XZ587 at RAF Valley
(Geoffrey Wedge – MOD/crown copyright)

2. 'Helicopter Rescue'

Following the publication of 'The Legend of Llandwrog' in 1994, the writer found it difficult in spite of promises to interest a television company in the birth of the RAF mountain rescue team at Llandwrog. The Air Ministry based the service on the organisation and exploits of this team. However, I was fortunate to make contact with BBC Wales commissioning producer, Judith Winnan. She put me in touch with Cwmni Da (Good Company) a television company based in Caernarfon, just prior to that company being given the commission to produce 'Helicopter Rescue'. I was taken on to include the story of birth of the RAF Llandwrog team.

On Armistice Day 2011 I took researcher/producer Angharad from the pipeline below Llyn Cowlyd on a track onto a heather moor with the intention of showing her the crash site of Avro Anson LT433 in which three of four aircrew had survived in 1944. Half way across I missed my footing on a boulder and went flying. 'Don`t worry' I called, to a worried Angharad, 'I learned to make parachute landings in the ATC – relax, and roll'. We continued to the line of low cliffs above which the Anson site lay. Lo and behold, a new fence had appeared topped by barbed wire. My companion had the sense to hold me back, though we could see several pieces of aluminium taunting us in the distance. A week later we were back with camerman Aled and set up to do an interview with the area of the crash site seen across a valley. Then an American fighter joined us and circled above. When the noisy intruder left we had then to wait until a council wagon and JCB passed by to carry out road repairs in this desolate spot! Part 1 'Helicopter Rescue' was transmitted on 15th February 2012 on BBC Wales and parts 2 and 3 succeeding weeks, and later on shown on BBC2 to a wider audience. The splendid Snowdonia National Park warden Brian Jones placed a stile over the barbed wire near Anson LT433 site for future walkers to view the parts of wreckage left. This was on his last day of service.

Interviewer Angharad & cameraman Aled of Cwmni Da, near outlet pipe of Llyn Cowlyd reservoir (Author)

3. Together Again

On 14th January 1943 Anson EG110 failed to clear Foel Grach at night returning from a flight to the Midlands. Pilot P/O Ken Archer, RNZAF, though injured covered his crew of three with parachutes and left the aircraft in the dark and in snow to get help. Seventeen hours later he found the remote farmhouse of Rowlyn Uchaf (Upper Whirlpool) and raised the alarm with farmer William Williams who raced to Tal y Bont post office to contact RAF Llandwrog. The Anson was not found until the next day, in spite of heroic efforts by the Llandwrog Mountain Rescue team, when only Sgt Paterson survived. Sgts Barnett RNZAF and Brocklehurst RAF had expired due to injuries and exposure.

Sgt (later P/O) Ken Archer (K. Archer)
Sgt Frank Paterson (Arthur Arculus)
Sgt Eric Brocklehurst (Laura Eccles)
Sgt William H. Barnett (Gwyn Hughes)

Sgt A. E. Clay in cockpit of Anson N4981
(Malcolm Short)

4. Low Flyer

Based at RAF Llandwrog, staff pilot Sgt A. E. Clay took off on 20th April 1942 in Anson N4981 with a crew of four Although he had already been warned about the perils of low flying he somehow found his aircraft over the village of Betws Garmon and because of cloud could not see the way ahead to Llyn Cwellyn via a narrow pass. He chose the only option then to obtain maximum power from the engines and charge up the valley leading to Moel Eilio. The Anson impacted high on the right side of the valley with the loss of all the crew.

5. Crash above Cowlyd

RAF Cark on the northern flank of Morecame Bay prepared pilots who would become staff pilots at Observers Advanced Flying Units. The pilots took it in turns to act as navigators on some flights. On the night of 20th February 1944 Sgt Bob Birch was acting as

ATC cadets of 418 (Aberconwy) Sqn examining wreckage of Anson LT433 above Llyn Cowlyd at Easter 1944 (Humphrey Smith via son Peter)

navigator on a flight to the south when Anson LT433 entered a snowstorm. Not realising that they were above the heart of Snowdonia he gave a course due north to the pilot Sgt Grant. The Anson struck a mountain near Craig Ffynnon where three of the four airmen survived to be found by a local farmer's son the next morning. The RAF Llandwrog Mountain Rescue team brought the crew members to safety in a long and difficult operation lasting into the next night. The pilot was the one fatality.

6. Halifax near Holywell

On 22nd February 1944 Halifax LK 626 of 431 Sqn took off from its base at Croft in Yorkshire on a day cross country exercise. When near Holywell the aircraft suffered failure of two of its engines and made a forced landing. None of the crew were injured, but the Halifax was written off. A local newspaper report said that it almost hit a bus as it was approaching the field where it landed.

Halifax LK640, sister ship of LK626 of 431 Sqn, Croft (David J Smith)

7. Kamloops to Allt y Ceffylau

The Merchant Ship Fighter Unit based at RAF Speke, near Liverpool, trained pilots to be catapulted from ships to repel attacks by enemy fighters – a one way operation. On 9th August 1942, Sgt Peter Riddoch and P/O Robert Bruce McIntyre took off from Speke to fly to RAF Valley for a week's gunnery practise. On the way they flew into cloud south of the coast. Riddoch realised they were above mountains. He spotted a funnel of light leading to a river (the Conway) and indicated to McIntyre to follow him, his radio being faulty. Riddoch followed the river to the coast and onto Valley. McIntyre's Hurricane P3385 struck the summit ridge of Allt y Cyffylau above lonely Llyn Cwmorthin, west of Blaenau Ffestiniog. A long way from Kamloops, British Columbia, where the pilot was from.

8. Lancaster at Dolwen Hill

On 16th November 1942, Lancaster W4326 was flying over mid Wales from its base with 101 Special Duties Squadron at Holme in Spalding Moor. At 0400 hours the tail was blown off by an explosion of a photo-flash in a rear fuselage chute. There was no chance for the crew to bale out. One of the seven lost was Sgt D. A. J. Holloway. He was 17 years old.

P/O Robert Bruce McIntyre
(Brenda Madigan – niece, via Mel Thomas)

Sgt D. A. J. Holloway
(Ray Holloway – nephew)

9. Lt Boyer's Medal

On 7th January 1944, USAAF B-24J Liberator 42-99991 flew into the hillside above Llanfairfechan. Lt Norman

P. C. Thomas John Thomas (Mrs Judith Raw – daughter)

Boyer managed to rescue Sgt Hal Alexander from his rear turret then pull a badly injured Sgt Lorenz from a waist gunner's window. He then went off to seek help, not from the coast but over a mountain, 2,000 feet Tal-y-Fan. Eventually, he came across the remote farmhouse of Waen Newydd above Rowen. The Roberts family looked after him until the ambulance arrived. PC Thomas John Thomas was the driver as well as a police officer. He rushed the injured airman to Llandudno Hospital.

Wings badge of Lt Norman Boyer (Mrs Judith Raw)

Boyer was so taken with the care he was given that he gave PC Thomas the wings badge off his uniform. Recently, PC Thomas' daughter Mrs Judith Raw, with the help of researcher Gwyn Hughes, returned the badge to Boyer's family in the shape of grandson Johnathon Wright, a police officer in Ohio.

10.   A Brace of Vampires

During the 1950's the main unit based at RAF Valley was No 7 Flying Training School with De Havilland

Vampires featuring twin booms and shrill sound of their Goblin engines. Lt J. B. Taylor, Royal Navy, took off from Valley on the afternoon of 3rd January 1957 on a clear bright day to carry out medium aerobatics south of Rhyl. Fourteen year old Huw Edwards was walking from Kinmel Bay towards Bodelwyddan to visit relatives at Fachell Farm when he observed Vampires doing aerobatics. 'The intention was to dive towards the ground at about 45 degrees, then level out.

At 1.15 p.m. One aircraft (WA417) failed to level out, went into the ground, and exploded. I ran to the crash site near Faenol Fawr Farm. The aircraft had disintegrated into fragments, large and small. The pilot had been killed instantly'.

Four engineers of British Gas were in the same field. At the very last moment the pilot managed to divert the Vampire from obliterating them to crash on the far side of the field.

The court of inquiry concluded that the pilot had lost control too near the ground to recover.

On 10th October 1958 a formation of Vampires was flying over the coast near Point of Ayr. One of the aircraft, WA394 flown by Lt J. Jmean of the Jordanian Air Force broke formation. It had run out of fuel, and the pilot was faced with landing it without injury to himself or the villagers below. First, he avoided the gas holder at Point of Ayr colliery by an estimated 20 feet. Keeping a cool head he next dived the aircraft under electricity cables, followed by swooping between two roadside bungalows only twenty yards apart. Then came a run through two hedges, hitting an electricity pole, and charging through a herd of cows, before coming to rest in a ditch. After climbing out of the

De Havilland Vampire XE874, one time gate guardian at RAF Valley
(Author)

Vampire WA394 near Talacre
(Gareth Pritchard – RAF Valley, MOD/crown copyright)

Vampire unhurt, Lt J. Jmean waved to the other pilots circling to see if he had survived. Soon, a 22 Sqn helicopter from RAF Valley landed and took him back to base. A guard was provided and fitters arrived to dismantle the aircraft over several days and return it to whence it came.

11. The Crimea Wellington

On 21st March 1941 Wellington R3288, B – Beer of 150 Sqn based at Newton, Notts took off to bomb submarine pens at Lorient on the Bay of Biscay. Over the English Channel a thick wad of cloud and a faulty radio deprived the crew of their position. The captain, F/O Elliott decided to jettison their bomb load and make a 180 degrees turn for base.

Much later and running short of fuel, the captain decided to reduce height from a safe 6,000 feet to 2,000 feet. They broke cloud at last above the railway shunting yards at Blaenau Ffestiniog. Shortly afterwards, climbing hastily, the aircraft struck the rocky knoll at the summit of the Crimea Pass. Four members of the crew lost their lives, but Sgt Peter Martlew the rear gunner survived when the turret broke off and rolled away.

For many years the wife of Sgt H. Beddall, the observer, made a visit to the

P/O Roland Clive Parkhurst, co-pilot (Patricia Colliss)

Sgt Harold Beddall, observer
(Mrs Beddall – wife)

Sgt John Killen air gunner
(Joseph Killen – brother via
Mel Thomas)

Memorial plaque to Wellington crew at St David's Church,
Blaenau Ffestiniog (Author)

Air cadets of no 2445 (Ardudwy) Sqn, Wing/Cdr Claire Short and Fl/Lt Carwyn Roberts – C/O (Author)

crash site to pay her respects to her husband and his crew. Sgt Peter Martlew was later promoted to Flight Lieutenant and flew as a radio observer in the Mosquitoes of 409 night fighter Sqn. When he passed away long after the war, his widow Margaret sent the writer treasured Christmas cards. They would always remind me of the Crimea Wellington and its crew.

12. A Wellington on Foel Grach

On 13th February 1943, Wellington HE466 based at 30 OTU, Hixon, near Stafford, took off on a cross country navigation exercise to the west. The aircraft flew into the upper slopes of Foel Grach in the Carneddau range, with the loss of its crew of five. They were:

Sgt Edward Frezell, RCAF, pilot.
P/O F. K. Thoroughgood, navigator.
Sgt C. G. Bennett, air gunner.
Sgt G. N. Rafferty, RCAF, wireless operator.
Sgt E. Towler, air gunner.

Sgt Edward Frezzell, pilot
(Nicole Mooney)

Sgt G. N. Rafferty, wireless operator
(Nicole Mooney)

The aircraft was found by chance the next day by Charles Driver, an Army officer training to carry out a mountain walk to the peaks. He recalled 'One of the crew was sitting up against a rock as if asleep. If only.'

13. The Bagillt Heinkel

On the evening of 7th May 1941, Heinkel He111, G1+LL was part of a force of enemy aircraft which bombed Liverpool docks. As the crew were a few minutes into their return journey they were suddenly attacked by a 256 Sqn Defiant night fighter flown by P/O D. Toone with F/O R. L. Lamb in the turret. Three airmen in the Heinkel were killed outright. The remaining crew members baled out. Pilot Lt Heinz Dunkerbeck landed in the Dee near Flint and observer Feldwebel Fritz Kitzing on the opposite side of the estuary at Parkgate.

14. A Close Shave

Pilot Officer Humphrey Smith, of 418 (Aberconwy) Sqn Air Training Corps was responsible, certainly in 1945-6, for handling the winch launches of gliders at No.63 WEGS at Tal-y-cafn, south of Conway.

A Home Guard stands by the tail fin of the Heinkel He111 on the Dee marshes (David J Smith)

Once in a while he would keep up his flying skills by taking a flight in a Kirby Cadet. We looked forward to an experienced pilot making a grand tour of the site, which would take some height. He took off and immediately went into a steep climb. The C/O, Flt/Lt Rich, was operating the winch.

Lt Heinz Dunkerbeck, pilot (H. Dunkerbeck)

Higher and higher soared the glider. Suddenly, there was a loud 'twang'. The cable had been stopped by the operator. Humphrey Smith was in a nose-up attitude at that moment so the glider stalled. All he could do was throw the control stick forward and drop the cable. The nose slowly went down and the glider picked up speed alarmingly. We gathered cadets held our breaths as the dive continued. We were expecting a shattering crash. At the very last moment the glider pulled out of the dive, only a matter of twenty feet or so above the field. We heard the swish

A Kirby Cadet awaiting take-off at Tal-y-cafn
(Peter Smith)

P/O Humphrey Smith, officer nearest the marching cadets of 418
(Aberconwy) Sqn ATC. Note U.S. Officer on saluting dias on
Llandudno promenade & U.S. Flag (Peter Smith – son)

of the wings, wondering why they did not fold. Then we remembered to breathe.

The glider landed by the winch and an unseemly row ensued as to why the pilot had not been allowed to release the cable in his own time and not been placed in such a precarious situation. At least he was spared to be able to continue launching his pupil cadets for the future.

15. The Hardest Walk

7th January 2015, David Bather of Penmaenmawr invited the author to pay our respects at the memorial to the Liberator crew members who lost their lives in 1944 at Moelfre above Llanfairfechan on the anniversary of the crash. We were joined by aviation researcher Steve Jones of Port Talbot.

Farmer Tecwyn took us up to the green track near Moelfre in his Landrover. When we climbed out we were hit by a wind of almost hurricane force. We had to walk bent at an angle of nearly 45 degrees.

I could not get my breath, and thought my heart would give out. Eventually with David pulling and Steve pushing, we reached the memorial, where I said a few words of

Author at Liberator memorial with David Bather (Steve Jones)

remembrance to the five airmen killed, and Booster their mascot.

A. Davis,
W. Lorenz,
W. Nichols,
S. Offutt,
N. Cennemo,
'Booster'

We were then blown back to the Landrover. Then down the mountain to hot cups of tea.

My hardest walk ever.